A MACDONALD BOOK

Translated by Judith Landry
English text editor Jenny Vaughan
English text consultant Michael Boorer

First published in Great Britain in 1987 by
Macdonald & Company (Publishers) Ltd
London & Sydney

A BPCC plc company

ISBN 0 356 11974 2

Printed and bound in Spain by Artes Gràficas,
Toledo S.A.
D. L. TO:1616 -1986

Macdonald & Company (Publishers) Ltd
Greater London House
Hampstead Road
London NW1 7QX

British Library Cataloguing in Publication Data

Piumini, Robert
Through the year.
1. Seasons—Juvenile literature
I. Title II. Pozzi, Gabriele
574.5′43 QH48

ISBN 0-356-11974-2

Through the Year

Roberto Piumini and Gabriele Pozzi

Illustrated by Gabriele Pozzi

Macdonald

Contents

A clockwork world

Have you ever looked inside a cuckoo clock? If you have, you'll know how there are cogs and wheels inside, which keep the clock running. There's a little door that opens every hour, and a little wooden bird that pops out and says 'cuckoo!'.

Whoever invented the cuckoo clock thought it was something new and unusual. But it wasn't really. The whole world is a bit like a clock, running smoothly all the time. Ever since life on earth began, each day of each week, each minute of each hour sees some new animal born, or a new flower opening, springing into life like the wooden bird in a cuckoo clock.

But these are real birds, mammals and insects, real fishes and flowers, which all have lives of their own. The little wooden cuckoo is really very dull in comparison: these real living things can do so much more than just say 'cuckoo!' every hour. The birds can fly and sing a whole chorus of songs. The insects buzz from flower to flower, the fishes swim in the deep cool water of lakes and streams. The mammals make their way through the woods and fields, and the trees, flowers and grass fill the air with their scent.

And, like a clock, all this works in a regular rhythm, from season to season through the months of the year.

January

In January, the snow falls, thick and deep, spreading over the world like a quilt on a bed.

Everything is white. The snowmen that the children have built stand proudly in their white kingdom. Even the sun above them is pale.

Two Christmas roses open their white petals. The centre of each flower is yellow, a bright contrast with the world around them.

'What's going on there?' grumble the snowmen. 'You two – close up those yellow eyes. Everything is supposed to be white in winter!'

The Christmas roses look nervously around them, and notice that the snowmen have carrot noses! But all the same, they feel a little scared by such a big, white world, and begin to close their petals again.

'Be brave, little friends,' says the holly that grows beside them. 'Let everyone see that lovely yellow! Look at me! I'm not afraid!'

And indeed it is true – for the holly has dark green leaves, and bright red berries that look like drops of blood. They stand out clearly against the pale sky.

'Look at me too! Look at me too!' sings the robin. 'Look at my red breast! Look how bright it is. I don't care about the snow!'

So the Christmas roses stay wide open, staring out across the cold, silent, snow.

February

Now it is February, and life is beginning to stir in the woods. Little clusters of snowdrops stretch upwards into the misty air. Under the forest floor, the young grass slowly comes to life, pushing its way through the soil and last year's dead leaves.

'Steady on,' they grumble. 'Let us sleep a bit longer . . . there's no rush. What will you do if there's another frost? Your stems will be killed off at once.'

But the new grass keeps on growing.

In the woods of the south, where it is warmer, the butterflies are just awake after their winter hibernation, stretching their wings in the February sunshine. All around them hang the long tassels of the pussy willow – showering one of the butterflies with pale pollen.

'It's making you look like a cabbage white,' laughs the other one, as it flies away, out of the wood.

January snows

January is a hungry time for animals. The hills and valleys are covered with snow, and it is hard for them to find anything to eat. Lakes and ponds freeze over so that the ducks and wading birds can no longer find food in and around the water.

A bird table

The little garden birds might envy the swallows and the other birds that fly away south to warmer lands. The robins, blackbirds, chaffinches, great tits and sparrows are all left behind, and must find food in the bleak countryside. You can help by putting out food for them. Make a bird table, and put crumbs and crusts on it. Give them mixed seeds too, and a few peanuts. They may not be able to say 'thank you' - but they will be grateful!

Winter courtship

Most animals like to find shelter in winter, and keep as warm as they can. But one kind of moth mates in winter. It does not live in Britain, but you can find it in southern Europe. Here you see the female (which has no wings) waiting for the male.

The first signs of spring

In February, we see the first signs that spring is on its way. The willow branches are covered with silver buds. In southern countries, the willow-warbler arrives and begins to look for a place to build a nest and rear a family. It will be a few more weeks before it reaches the northern woods.

The first butterflies appear too – but only in the warmer south. Further north, these pretty creatures are still hibernating, and will not wake until warmer days arrive.

Animal tracks

The snow begins to melt, and the ground is soft and muddy. The earliest spring flowers can be seen – the snowdrops and, here and there, the first violets. You can hear songbirds: the blackbirds, thrushes and robins. There is still frost at night, and the ground is hard and icy in the mornings. It is a good time to see animal tracks. Look for signs of the fox, the weasel, the stoat and the hare.

March

The new grass has pushed its way through the soil, and the ground is green and fresh again. The branches of the trees are covered with new buds, gradually unfolding in the spring sunshine.

A lark sings high above a meadow, while far below, the primroses blossom under the hedgerows.

'I wish we could sing like you,' they murmur.

'But you are a lovely colour,' the lark replies. 'Look how dull I am.'

'But you can fly,' say the shy violets. 'And we can never do that.'

At once, the air is full of laughter. Only the old chestnut leaf, left over from last year, is sad.

'I am no colour at all any more . . . ' it sighs.

'Then fly!' cries the lark and lifts it high into the air, and then lets it free to wheel and float in the strong March wind.

April

Now there are flowers almost everywhere. The cherry tree is in bloom, with pink and white flowers hanging in bunches among the red-striped leaves. The daffodils beneath it nod in the breeze.

The bees buzz around the cherry tree, each one seeking out a blossom.

'What do you want?' ask the puzzled flowers.

'Your nectar, of course. We always want nectar,' the bees reply.

'Why should we let you have it?' ask the flowers.

'Well, everything in the world has to take from other things,' explain the bees. 'The tree you're growing on takes goodness from the soil and the rain and the sunshine. And we must take the nectar, because we cannot live without it.'

They tell the cherry blossom about their hive, and the golden palace they have built there which we call a honey comb. They tell them about the honey they make, that is so sweet that everyone wants it – and how they need nectar to make it. So the flowers give up their nectar, just as they do every year.

Spring is here!
The birds know it is time to build nests and start families. The males begin by singing. They do this to attract mates, and to tell other male birds to keep away.

A blackbird's nest is made of twigs and clay. It is cup-shaped and rather roughly built. We can sometimes find these nests in hedgerows and bushes.

The chaffinch takes more care. It builds a neat, round nest in the fork of a tree, and covers it with moss. The female sits on four or five eggs, and after a couple of weeks these hatch. Then both parents care for the new-born fledgelings.

Colour everywhere
The woods are carpeted with primroses. Butterflies appear, such as the yellow brimstone. The orange tip has just emerged from its chrysalis. It has spent all winter changing from a caterpillar to a butterfly.

April flowers

The fruit trees are laden with pink and white blossom. Along the hedgerows we find red and white dead-nettles, blue forget-me-nots and golden dandelions. The bees buzz to and fro, collecting nectar and pollen to make honey – and as they do so, they help the flowers by fertilizing them. This makes it possible for the seeds to form, so the plants can reproduce.

The hunters awake

As the April sunshine warms the earth, the frogs, toads and lizards wake from their winter hibernation. They come out of the muddy ditches and the cracks in the old stone walls – out into the warm sun.

The frogs croak in chorus. They too will mate and lay eggs. Each female frog can lay up to 4000 eggs, every one of them wrapped in a kind of jelly to protect it. But not all those eggs will end up as adult frogs. They hatch into tadpoles – which have plenty of enemies among birds and fishes. And by the time they have become young frogs, the grass snake too may be lying in wait, ready to catch them unawares.

May

The dog rose is in bloom, filling the air with its scent. A rose chafer sits on a flower, nibbling at the petals. Its glistening green-gold body gleams in the sun.

'Aren't you afraid someone will see you – all shiny like that?' asks a timid rabbit, crouching in the grass. The little animal's pale brown fur blends perfectly with its background, so it can hardly be seen.

'What should I be afraid of?' asks the young chafer. 'I'm armour plated, no one can hurt me.'

'I envy you,' whispers the rabbit. 'I'm afraid of everyone.'

'Well, we're safer than you'd think,' says another chafer. 'It's hard to see us when we're among the green leaves. But these petals . . . they're really worth taking a risk for!'

June

It's a warm, still afternoon, peaceful and silent. The laburnum trees are in full bloom – their long bunches of flowers hang low over the garden path.

Suddenly there's a loud bang! It's a noise like a thunderclap – and very close.

The little blackcap starts in fright.

'What was that?' it asks the white admiral butterfly.

'It's a farmer, shooting pigeons,' the butterfly replies. 'I'd stay out of the way if I were you!'

'You're right – I think I will,' says the blackcap, and flies away through the trees.

Maybugs

May is the time for maybugs or *cockchafers.* They live among the forest trees – the oaks and beeches, whose leaves they love to eat. Maybugs were once very common, and did a lot of damage. But today, there are not many woodlands left, and people use insecticides - so the maybug finds it hard to survive. One day it may vanish for ever.

The maybug spends the first three or four years of its life underground, feeding on roots. Then it becomes a pupa, and finally hatches into a maybug.

Every three or four years, we find there are far more maybugs than usual. This is because once the eggs are laid, they take three or four years to develop from larvae into adult beetles.

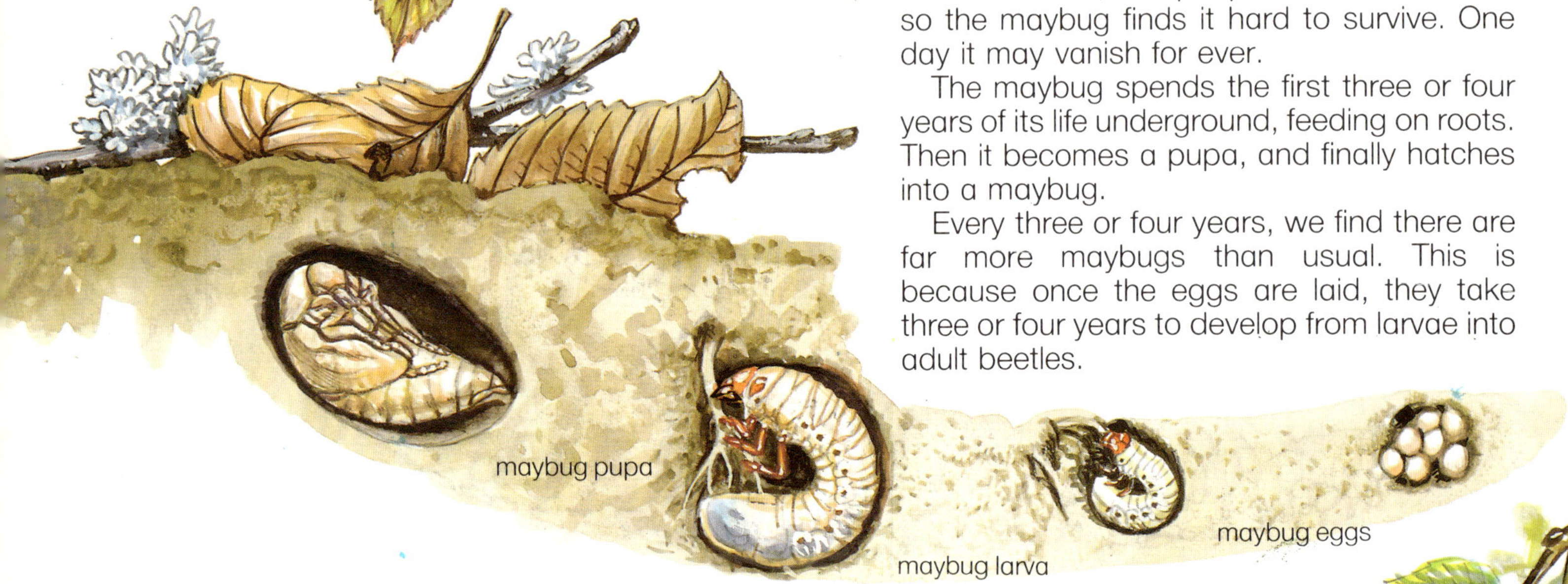

In the wood

In the shade of the woodland trees, the mother deer gives birth to her fawn. Its spotted coat matches the dappled sunlight, making it hard to see. We call this *camouflage.* It is a way in which animals protect themselves from enemies.

Our fields and gardens are full of flowers, while sweet-smelling lilies of the valley bloom in the woods.

Loudly sing cuckoo!

Everyone knows what the cuckoo sounds like. We can hear it calling on a summer afternoon – but we hardly ever see the cuckoo. It hides deep in hedges and thickets, making itself impossible to find.

The cuckoo flies to Europe every summer from Africa. The female looks for the nest of another bird and lays her own egg in it. She never makes a nest of her own. When the young cuckoo hatches, the bird that made the nest will feed it. The young cuckoo throws the other eggs out, so it gets all the care and attention for itself.

Along the hedgerows

In June, the hops begin to ripen. The green flower-like cones of the female plant are used in making beer. They give it its flavour. In some places, farmers grow whole fields of hops. But these plants also grow wild, climbing over the other plants along our hedgerows.

At sunset, you may see white male moths near these hedges, like tiny ghosts. And that is what they are called – ghost moths. Their caterpillars live in the soil, nibbling the roots of the hop plants.

July

July is often the hottest month of the year. The sun beats down on the ripening corn, and the scarlet poppies nod to the sparrows.

'Don't you think we are beautiful? So red – you can see us miles away.'

The corn shimmers like a golden sea, and the deep blue cornflowers wave gently to and fro.

'Look at us,' they seem to say. 'As blue as the sky, bluer than cool water. So much more restful than red, don't you think?'

The sparrows flit through the corn, settling here and there. They cling to the ears of corn with their slender feet, and peck away at the golden grains.

August

It is a still hot night, and there is a scent of honeysuckle in the air.

'Why aren't you singing, nightingale?' ask the flowers. 'It's been a long time since we heard your song – and it's so beautiful.'

'It's too late in the year,' the nightingale tells them. 'Look at the sky! How far away the stars are! I'd sing to them, if there were a little closer.'

And then the air is full of falling stars, tumbling down to hear the nightingale. But the nightingale still does not sing.

Night music in July

In summer the night is full of sounds. If you listen carefully, you may hear the love-call of the male crickets. They do not make this sound with their voices – they make it with their wings. They rub them together, like a bow on a violin. They make this sound to attract the females who will be their mates.

After mating, the female lays her eggs and pushes them into the soil, using a small, pointed tube she has at the end of her body. This is called an *ovipositor.*

Insects and insect eaters

In July, when so many flowers bloom, the insects breed. They lay their eggs, which hatch out into thousands of young. If it were not for insect eaters, there might be nothing left of the plants that grow in our countryside.

There are many birds that eat insects. Warblers, swallows and woodpeckers all depend on them for food.

The woodpecker has its own special way of catching its food. It uses its strong beak to make a hole in the bark of a tree. Then it pecks out the insects and insect larvae it finds underneath, using its long tongue to catch them.

August voices

Down in the south of Europe, we can hear the cicada sing. This insect spends most of its life as a larva. It lives underground, and has feet shaped like spades, which it uses for digging.

When they are adults, cicadas come out into the sunshine. In August they sit in trees, singing to their future mates. They all sing together – and the noise can be very loud indeed!

The cicada makes its sound by vibrating two membranes under its body. (A membrane is like a thin sheet.) It also has a sound box under its body. This makes the noise louder. We say it *amplifies* it.

Radar signals

As evening falls, the bats come out from their roosts, where they have been sleeping through the day.

At night they fly about in the dark, giving out squeaking sounds. These are so high-pitched that humans cannot hear them. The sounds bounce off anything in their path, echoing back to the bat. The bat can use these echoes to tell exactly where an object is. And if that object is an insect, it stands little chance of survival, for the bat will hunt it down and eat it.

September

September has arrived, and summer is almost over. There are still a few flowers here and there, along the bank of the stream. But the leaves are already beginning to turn brown. The dragonfly perches, quite still, among the reeds.

'What's happening to the summer?' the young frog asks the old one. 'Where's it going?'

'Who knows?' croaks the old frog. 'Who knows?'

'I'm going to look for it!' says the young frog, diving into the water. The old frog does not follow – it simply stares at the sky, keeping quite still. Soon it will be time to dive to the bottom of the pond, and sleep there all through the winter, buried under the mud.

October

By October, the year is old, and the leaves turn golden brown. But down on the woodland floor, there are new plants pushing their way through the soil and out into the air. They are autumn crocuses, with long, pink-tipped petals.

'Look at us, we're new!' they say.

'But not for long,' say the old alder leaves. 'We were new once, but now we're tired, and full of holes. Soon we'll fall from this tree and lie there with all the other dead leaves that you can see.'

'That suits us!' say the field mushrooms. 'There's nothing we like better than dead leaves. We feed on them all the time, and we grow bigger and bigger! Oh yes, there's nothing better than a few dry leaves.'

All this time, the dormouse sits quietly on a low bough of the alder tree. Its bright eyes stare at the pink crocus flowers. 'How pretty they are!' it sighs.

September – it's time to leave

When September comes, the ducks and wading birds gather together in large groups in marshy areas. They will soon be off to Africa, where the climate is warmer. At this season you may see groups of tufted ducks resting between stages of their long journey.

Hawk moths at twilight

In the evening, the air is full of the scent of flowers. This is the time when the moths appear, almost like ghosts in the dusk. Among these are the hawk moths.

The moths fly through the darkness, and now and then hover above the flowers, fluttering their wings very fast.

A moth has a special kind of tongue for reaching the nectar in a flower. This is called a *proboscis*. It is a long tube which the moth can use to suck up the nectar. The proboscis is so long that the moth does not even need to land on the flower in order to reach the nectar.

The thistle and its friends

It might seem as if the thistle has reached the end of its useful life. It is hard, dry and dead. But this is the time when the goldfinches like it best – for it is full of seeds they like to eat. All through Europe we can see them, fluttering among the thistles in September.

October woods

The squirrel is getting ready for the winter. It is busy, collecting a store of nuts, pine seeds and acorns. The squirrel does not hibernate, so it tries to be sure it has collected enough food to last the winter.

Recognizing fungi

There are plenty of fungi growing in the autumn woods. Some are safe to eat – but take care, for others are poisonous.

The fly agaric is one of the most dangerous – yet it is also very beautiful. You should not pick the fungi, however lovely they look – for they are as valuable as rare flowers.

If you gather edible mushrooms, take care how you do it. If you look at the ground the mushrooms come from, you might see a mass of threads there. This is called the *mycelium*. Take care not to harm it. New mushrooms will grow from the mycelium when *spores* from the ripe ones reach it. Spores are like fine powder, under the cap of the mushroom.

November

There's a rustling sound on the woodland floor. It is a little brown and grey bird, hopping nervously through the leaves. It lowers its head, and its short tail points straight upwards to the sky.

'What's the matter, little wren?' asks the ivy.

'I was carrying a seed in my beak,' explains the wren, still searching among the leaves. 'And I dropped it. I was going to eat it, but now I can't find it anywhere.'

'Never mind, little bird,' says the ivy. 'It won't be wasted. It'll lie there under the leaves until spring, and then it will grow into a new plant. And that new plant will have many more seeds – for you and lots of other birds.'

But the little wren still goes on looking for a while.

'Oh dear,' it sighs. 'Now I'm so tired and thirsty . . . Let me drink some of those drops of water you hold on your leaves, ivy plant.'

'Of course, little friend,' says the ivy plant.

December

Now the snow has come again. It lies between the roots of the trees and weighs heavily on the branches. A splash of dark green ivy stands out from the whiteness all around.

The wintry wood is silent. But there is more life there than you think. Hidden from sight, animals sleep the winter away, hibernating until spring comes round again. The snail clings to an underground root, dreaming of the summer. In its dream, it talks to a butterfly.

'Do you remember the summer?' it sighs. 'It was so lovely, when the grass was green and the flowers bloomed. And the earth smelled so lovely after a summer storm!' The butterfly has its own dream – of cornfields and poppies, and deep blue cornflowers.

The dormouse too is curled up in its nest, dreaming of the sunshine and the long days of summer, so far away.

Gabriele Pozzi

The countryside in November

There is little colour about in November – except for the ripening holly berries. They are brilliant red, and give a welcome touch of brightness to the winter scene. The birds welcome the berries too, for there is not much else to eat at this time of year.

Winter sleepers

Now many of the trees are quite bare, for all their leaves have fallen to the ground. There they turn brown and rot away to form *humus*, which makes the soil rich and fertile. There are seeds on the ground too – which animals like the dormouse are glad to find.

This tiny rodent loves nuts and eats as much as it can before it begins its winter hibernation. It spends the winter in a burrow beneath the ground, but in summer it makes its nest of moss and twigs in a hedgerow. This is where it rears its young.

The watchman of the December woods

The owl goes on hunting all through the winter, however hard the frost. It has bright eyes, with which it can see in the dark, and tufts of feathers on its head that look like ears.

You can see where an owl has its favourite tree, because there will be *owl pellets* beneath it. These are little balls of hair, feathers and bones. They are parts of the creatures it eats, which it cannot digest. The owl *regurgitates* these (forces them back up its throat) after it has eaten its prey.

Winter clothes

In winter, white snow covers the ground. Animals with brown coats would be easy to see – so many of them change colour to match the snow.

In places where winters are always snowy, there are animals that turn white in winter. There is a partridge in the Alps that does this. Its colour merges with the colour of the snow, so that *predators* (hunting animals) find it hard to see.

The stoat too can change colour – but it only does this when it lives in snowy places, such as the far north. Its white coat helps it hunt for food. Its prey cannot see it against the snow.